The Climate Crisis

ANIMAL EXTINCTIONS

A Graphic Guide

Stephanie Loureiro
illustrated by Ash Stryker

Graphic Universe™ • Minneapolis

Graphic Universe™
An imprint of Lerner Publishing Group, Inc.
241 First Avenue North
Minneapolis, MN 55401 USA

For reading levels and more information, look up this title at www.lernerbooks.com.

Main body text is set in Dave Gibbons Lower. Typeface provided by Comicraft.

Library of Congress Cataloging-in-Publication Data

Names: Loureiro, Stephanie, author. | Stryker, Ash, illustrator.
Title: Animal extinctions : a graphic guide / written by Stephanie Loureiro ; illustrated by Ash Stryker.
Description: Minneapolis : Graphic Universe, [2023] | Series: The climate crisis | Includes bibliographical references and index. | Audience: Ages 8–12 | Audience: Grades 4–6 | Summary: "Rising temperatures around the globe put animals at risk. They lose their homes. They lose food and water sources. Find out more about animal conservation and what people are doing to prevent animal extinctions"— Provided by publisher.
Identifiers: LCCN 2023010113 (print) | LCCN 2023010114 (ebook) | ISBN 9781728476902 (library binding) | ISBN 9798765623466 (paperback) | ISBN 9798765613023 (epub)
Subjects: LCSH: Extinct animals—Pictorial works—Juvenile literature. | Wildlife conservation—Juvenile literature. | BISAC: JUVENILE NONFICTION / Animals / Endangered
Classification: LCC QL88 .L68 2023 (print) | LCC QL88 (ebook) | DDC 591.68—dc23/ eng/20230316

LC record available at https://lccn.loc.gov/2023010113
LC ebook record available at https://lccn.loc.gov/2023010114

Manufactured in the United States of America
1 – CG – 7/15/23

TABLE OF CONTENTS

Adélie Penguins

Adélie penguins were mid-sized birds with black-and-white feathers. They were native to the Antarctic region, which was once covered in ice and had below-freezing temperatures. They were first discovered in 1840 due to rapid increases in Antarctic temperature caused by global climate change. This led to the destruction of their once-frozen habitat. The Adélie penguin became extinct in 2035.

Extinct means a species no longer exists. Dinosaurs became extinct a long time ago. People can only learn about them through books, fossils, and museums. Many living animals face the same possibility.

Climate change puts countless animals at risk. Because of rising global temperatures, they lose food and water sources as well as their habitats. Scientists have predicted that by the year 2070, between 16 and 30 percent of known animal species will become extinct.

I work for IUCN, the International Union for Conservation of Nature. I help keep track of where animals fall on the Red List. Has anyone ever heard of the Red List before?

CAREER DAY

All are welco here

The Red List gives each animal, plant, and fungus a category. This way, scientists can know how much danger a living thing might be in.

What kind of categories are there?

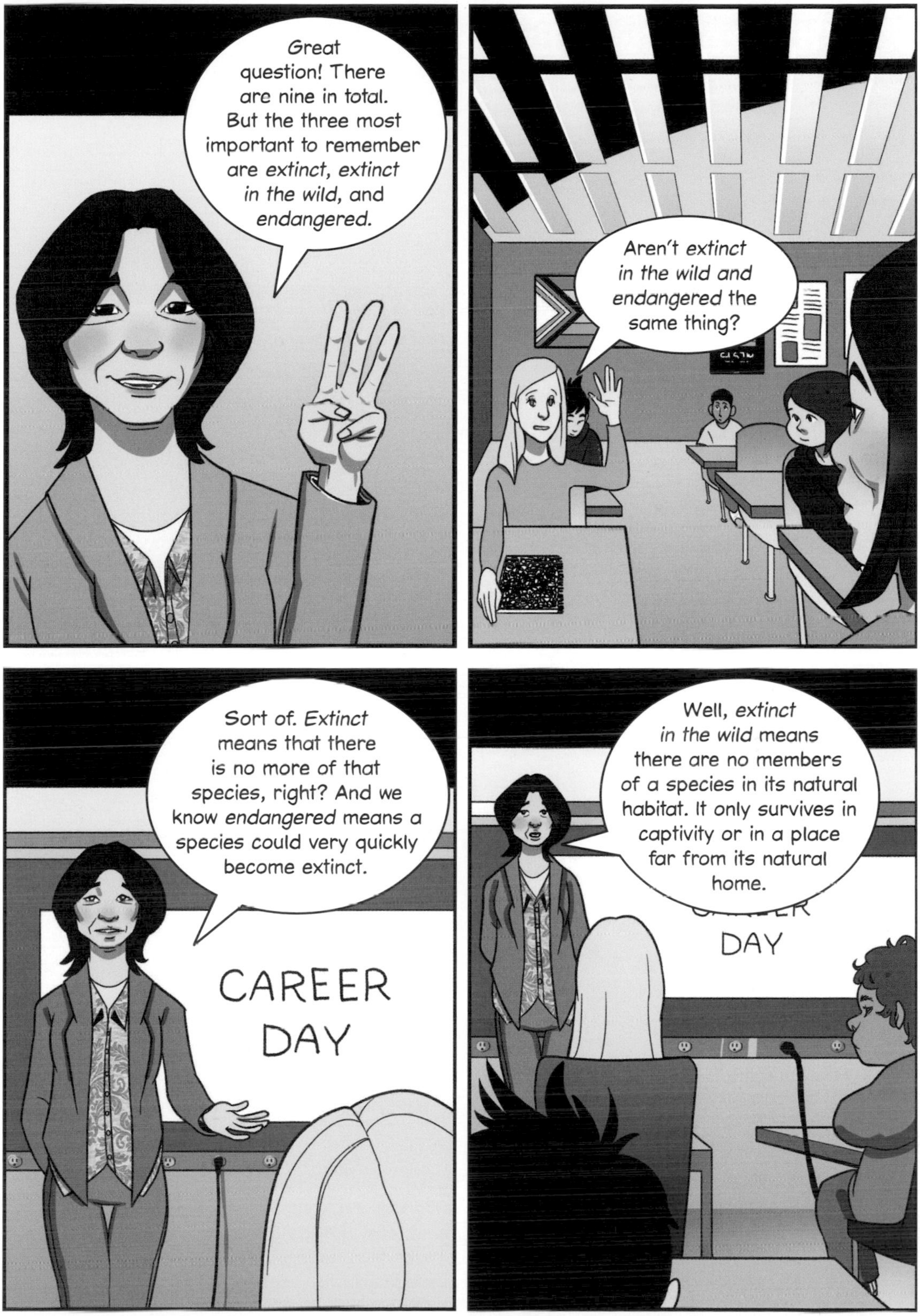
Great question! There are nine in total. But the three most important to remember are *extinct*, *extinct in the wild*, and *endangered*.
Aren't *extinct in the wild* and *endangered* the same thing?
Sort of. *Extinct* means that there is no more of that species, right? And we know *endangered* means a species could very quickly become extinct.
CAREER DAY
Well, *extinct in the wild* means there are no members of a species in its natural habitat. It only survives in captivity or in a place far from its natural home.
DAY

Many people hear the word *extinct* and think of dinosaurs. They are the most famous example. But another extinction was even worse. It's called the Permian extinction, and it happened 250 million years ago.

The Permian extinction began with a series of volcanoes erupting. The volcanoes let out huge amounts of ash and a greenhouse gas called carbon dioxide. The releases caused a warming much like modern global warming. Temperatures were rising everywhere, including in the oceans.

Scientists studied fossils of marine life from this period. They found that the rising temperatures meant that marine animals couldn't breathe. The water did not contain enough oxygen for all of them.

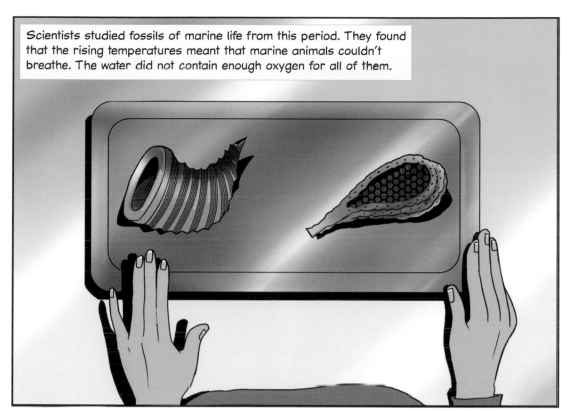

The Permian extinction and modern global warming have one major thing in common: habitat destruction.

Hi, sweetie. How's your research on polar bears going?

Not great. I found something that said climate change is causing the ice caps to melt. And that means polar bears' habitats could be destroyed.

Then I started to read more about how climate change harms animals. Did you know that when the ocean gets too warm, fish and other animals can't survive anymore?

There are droughts too. Animals might not get enough water. The plants they eat can't grow.

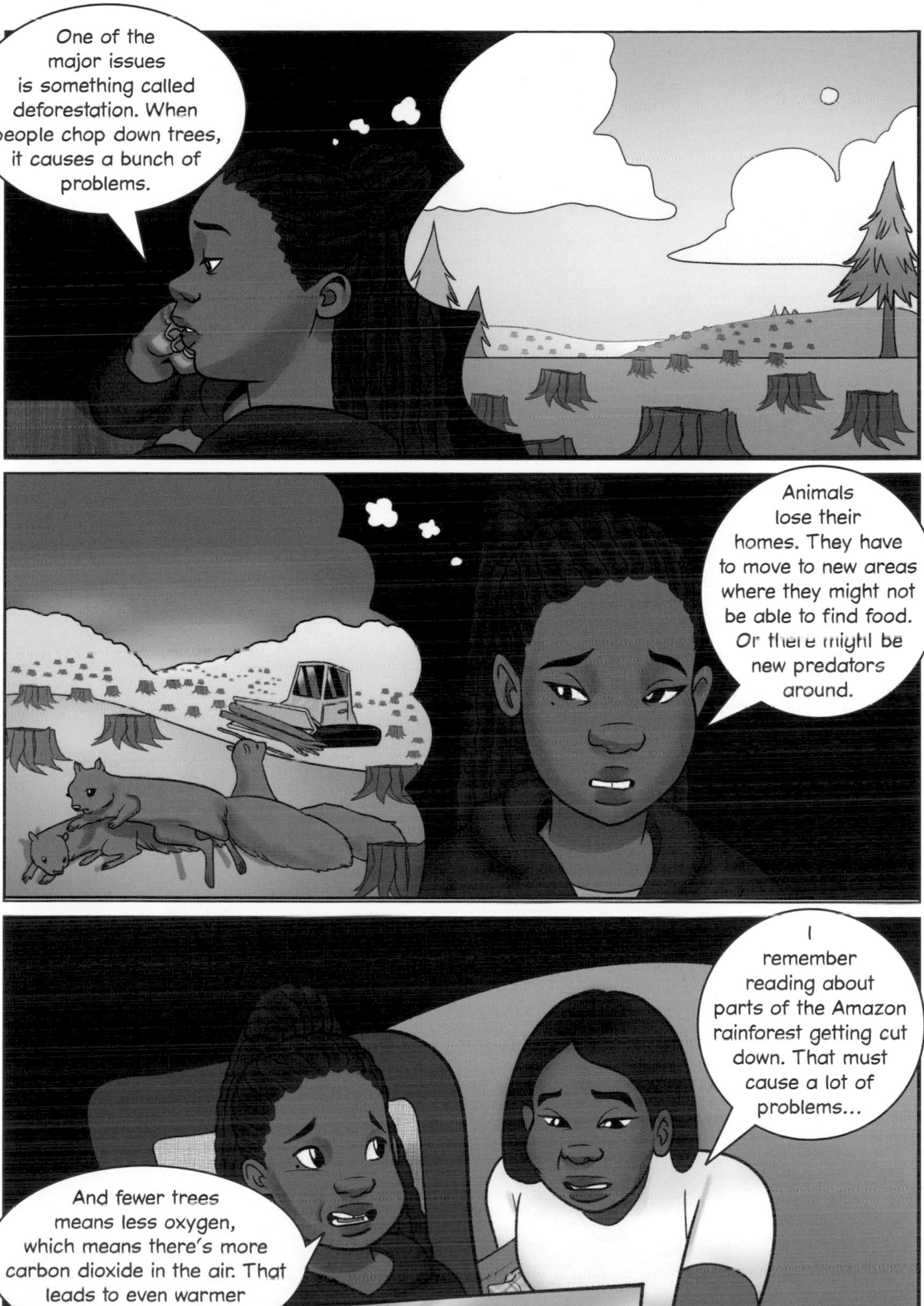
One of the major issues is something called deforestation. When people chop down trees, it causes a bunch of problems.
Animals lose their homes. They have to move to new areas where they might not be able to find food. Or there might be new predators around.
I remember reading about parts of the Amazon rainforest getting cut down. That must cause a lot of problems...
And fewer trees means less oxygen, which means there's more carbon dioxide in the air. That leads to even warmer temperatures!

I saw a video about that.

The Amazon rainforest is the largest in the world. It's home to more than 40,000 tree species alone. New species of plants and animals are being discovered every year.

Amazon Deforestation | 2023 Documentary

The Amazon is sometimes called the "lungs of the earth." The trees in the rainforest "breathe" out oxygen. They also absorb 2.2 billion tons* of carbon dioxide. That carbon dioxide would be heating up the planet otherwise.

*2 billion metric tons

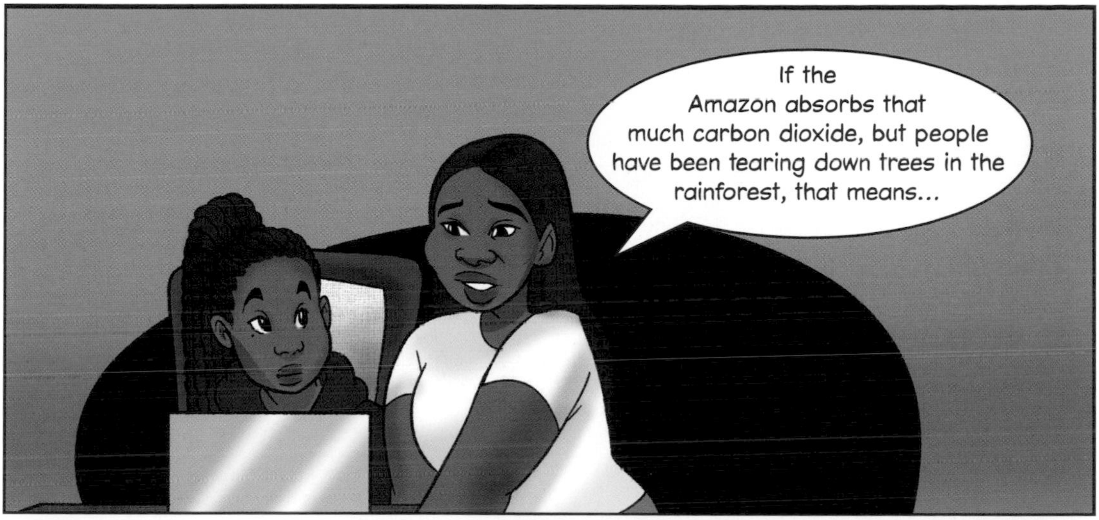
If the Amazon absorbs that much carbon dioxide, but people have been tearing down trees in the rainforest, that means...

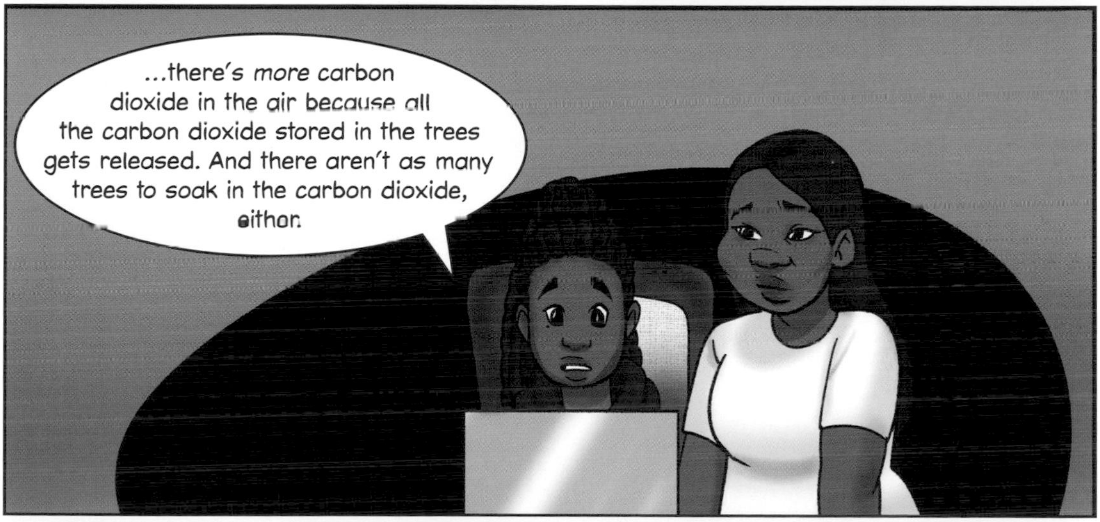
...there's *more* carbon dioxide in the air because all the carbon dioxide stored in the trees gets released. And there aren't as many trees to soak in the carbon dioxide, either.

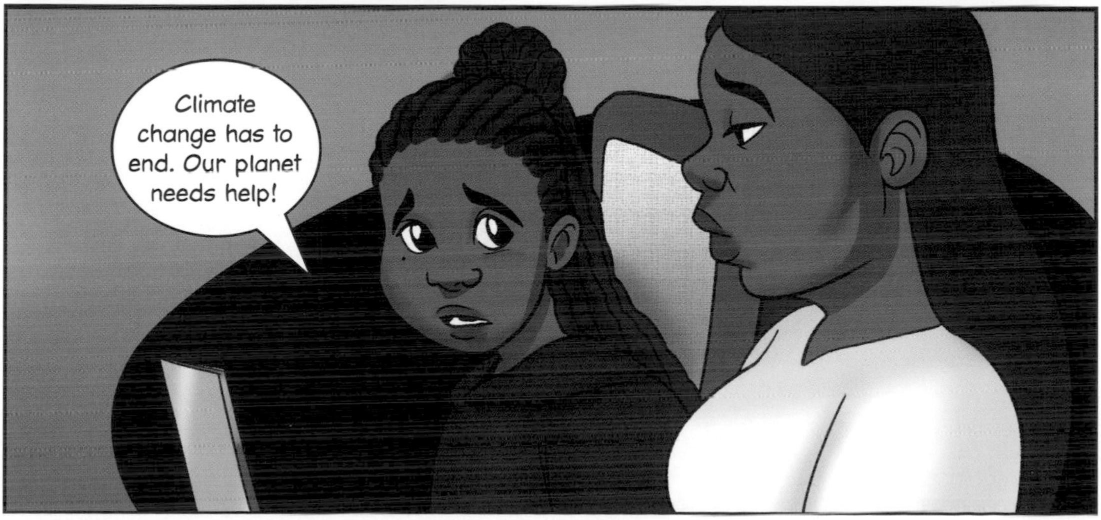
Climate change has to end. Our planet needs help!

Conservationists are working to help animals and plants that climate change has put at risk.

An endangered species called the Bramble Cay melomys lived on a tiny island in Australia. These rats were on the verge of extinction.

In 2014, a survey group found only 12 rats on the island. Rising sea levels caused flooding, leaving it completely underwater. In 2019, the rodent became the first known mammal to go extinct due to modern climate change.

For decades, people in Australia cleared koala habitats to make room for cities. In 2019 and 2020, weather events driven by climate change made the situation worse. Brush fires destroyed more of the habitats. Koalas went from "vulnerable" to "endangered" in just one decade.

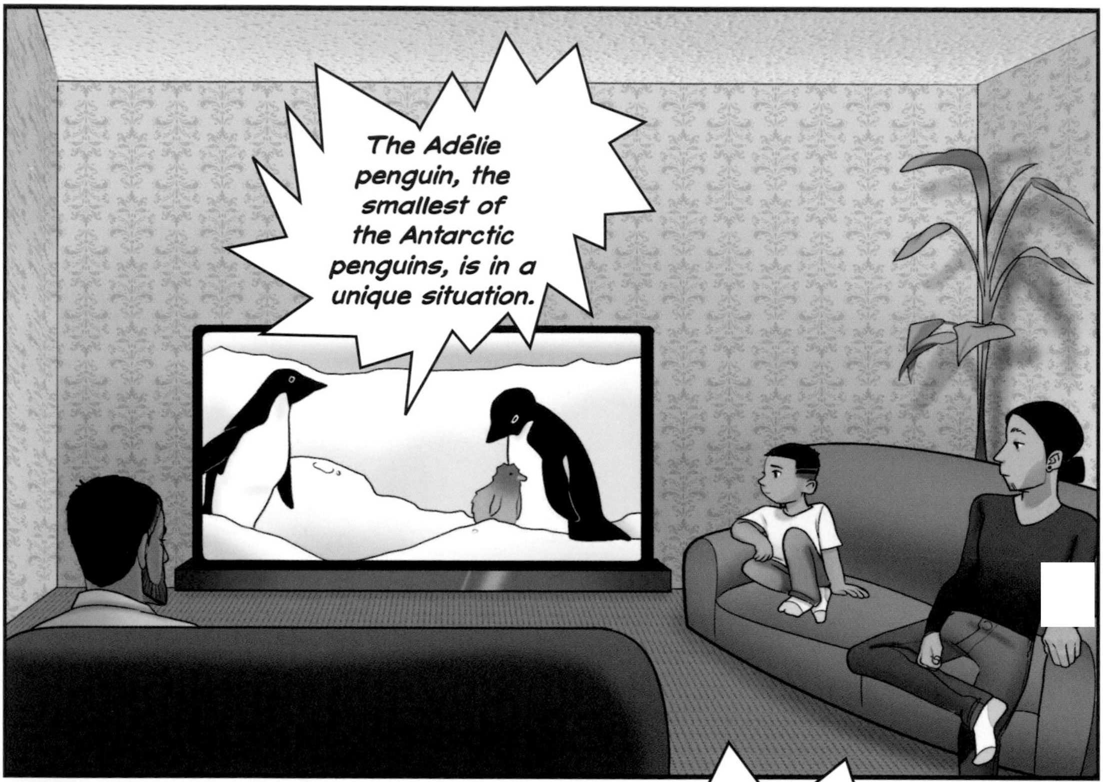
The Adélie penguin, the smallest of the Antarctic penguins, is in a unique situation.

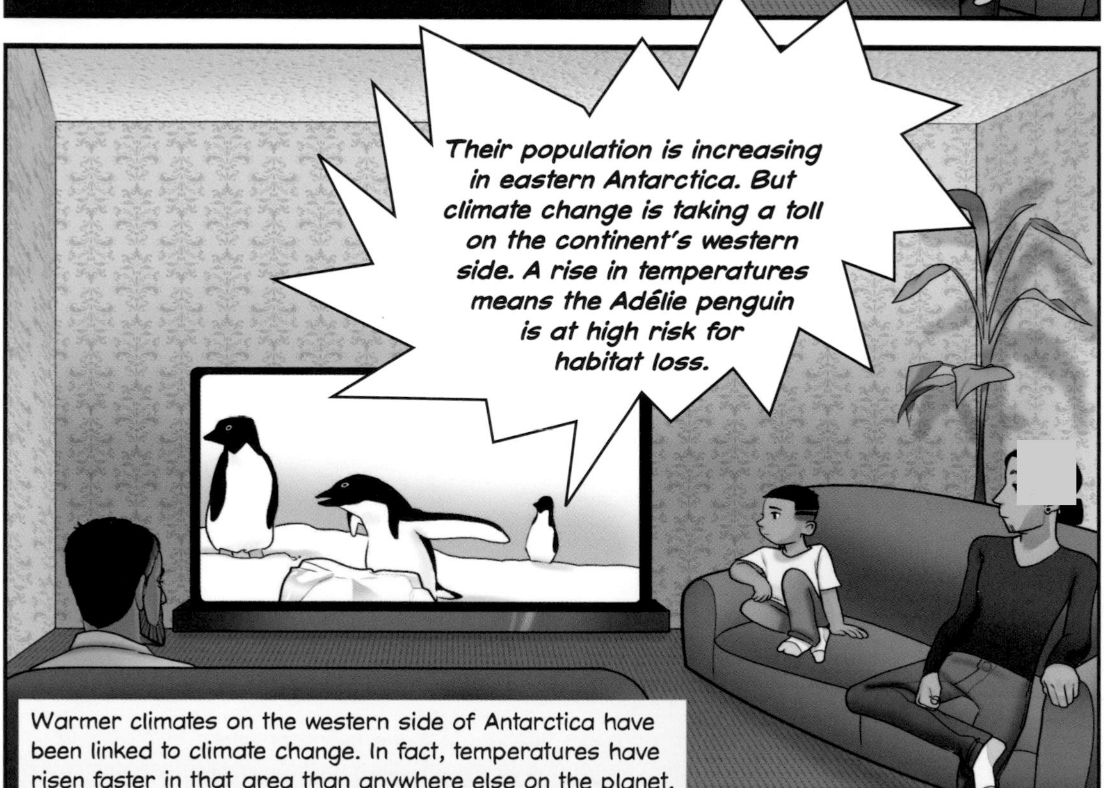
Their population is increasing in eastern Antarctica. But climate change is taking a toll on the continent's western side. A rise in temperatures means the Adélie penguin is at high risk for habitat loss.
Warmer climates on the western side of Antarctica have been linked to climate change. In fact, temperatures have risen faster in that area than anywhere else on the planet.

It's a harsh reality for many animals who live in Earth's cold polar regions. On the other side of the globe, the Arctic polar bear has also been harmed by rising temperatures.

Polar bears need sea ice to hunt and breed. But carbon dioxide emissions have made their habitats too warm. The water is heating up and the ice is melting, which makes hunting for prey more difficult.

Scientists have said that if people don't limit the rise in average global temperature, polar bears could be extinct by the year 2100.

No! I love polar bears! Grandma gave me a stuffed one when I was little. Remember?

Dad, can we find a way to help?

The ocean affects our entire climate. In fact, a livable climate depends on it. It is our responsibility to care for the ocean as well as our climate. And we are not doing enough of either.

10 Years Ago

Present

Global carbon emissions have caused rising ocean temperatures. When this happens, marine life is in trouble. Coral bleaching is one example.

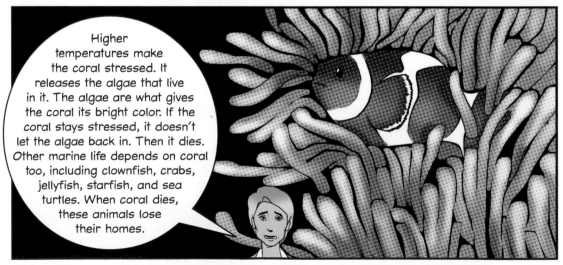

Higher temperatures make the coral stressed. It releases the algae that live in it. The algae are what gives the coral its bright color. If the coral stays stressed, it doesn't let the algae back in. Then it dies. Other marine life depends on coral too, including clownfish, crabs, jellyfish, starfish, and sea turtles. When coral dies, these animals lose their homes.

Speaking of sea turtles, banning single-use plastic bags and straws is not enough to help save them.

Sea turtles lay their eggs in the sand. The sand's temperature plays a role in the sex of the turtles. If it is below 81.9° Fahrenheit*, the hatchlings will be male. Above 88.8° F** and they will be female. When the temperature is in between, the turtles will be mixed. Scientists have found that if temperatures keep rising, there will be far more females than males.

And due to rising sea levels, the beaches where the turtles lay these eggs may not even be around.

*27.7° Celsius **31.6° C

Monarch butterflies use temperature as a signal that tells them when to migrate, hibernate, and reproduce. They end up traveling between 2,000 and 3,000 miles* every year.

The butterflies migrate from Canada and the United States down to Mexico every autumn. People often call this the great monarch migration.

The butterflies hibernate in Mexican forests. But climate change has caused warmer temperatures in both their hibernation and summer breeding areas. This puts the butterflies at risk because they cannot hibernate.

Along with warmer temperatures, the increased use of herbicides has led to less milkweed. This plant is the only place where monarch butterflies will lay their eggs.

*3,219 and 4,828 km

Cheetahs have faced extinction before due to poaching. But the threat of climate change may put them at even greater risk.

Severe droughts in eastern and southern Africa, where cheetahs live, have made drinking water harder to find. Cheetahs' hunting grounds are also being lost because humans are using these lands for farming.

Chapter Three: Survival through Adaptation

While climate change is a threat to many species, certain creatures have adapted. Scientists say that animals have "shapeshifted" to deal with warmer temperatures. Some have developed longer beaks or limbs to help reduce body heat.

 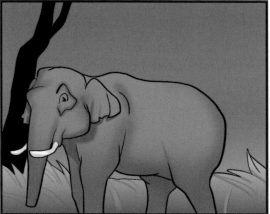

An African elephant's ears are larger than those of the Asian elephant. The African elephant's habitat is also sunnier. Temperatures are higher. Elephants flap their ears to get rid of some body heat. Bigger ears have more surface area, which means they move more air with each flap.

 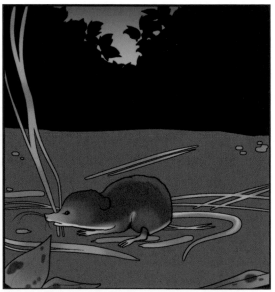

Some animals evolved to have longer tails. Wood mice and shrews are two examples. Like the elephants' ears, longer tails help lower body temperatures more easily.

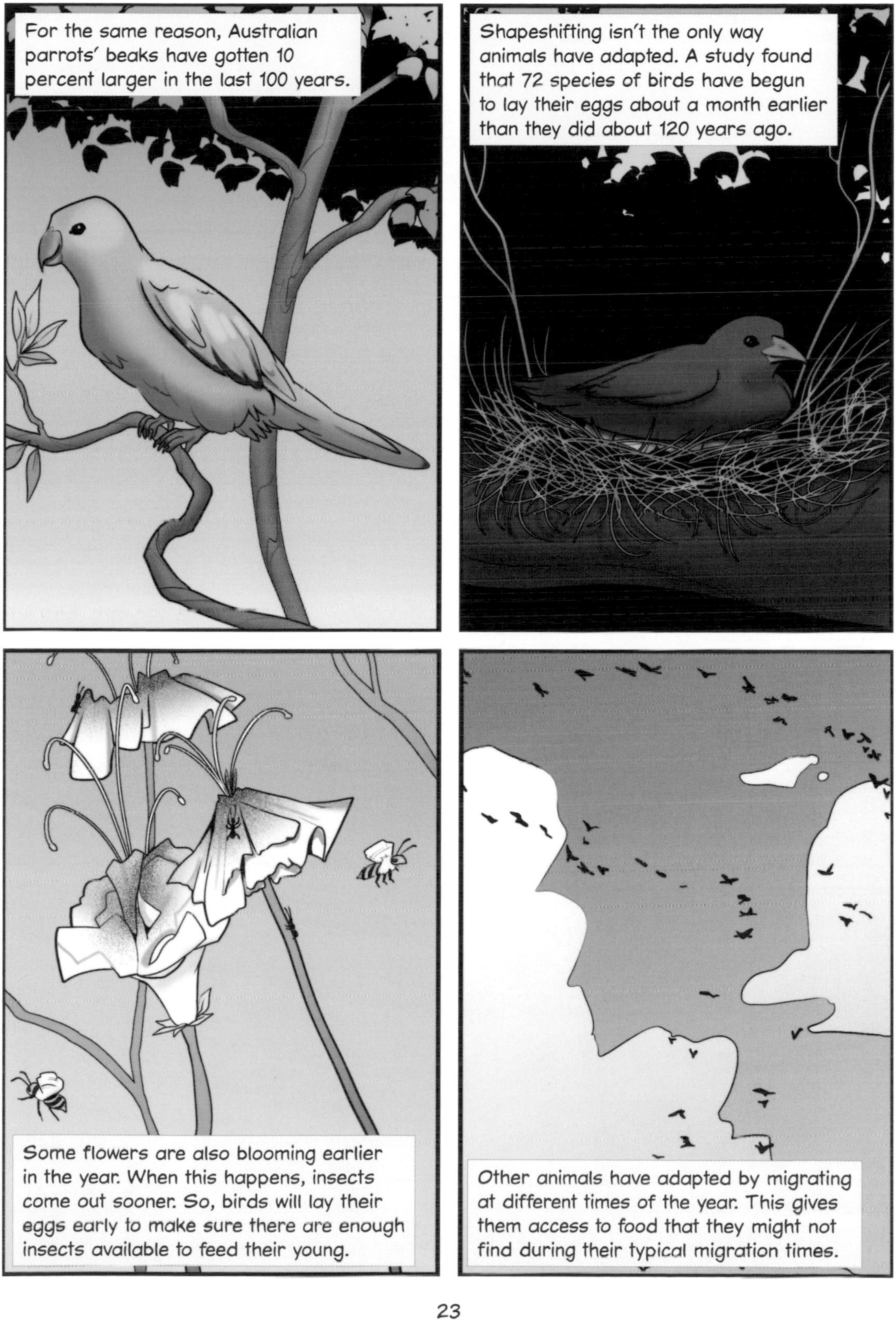
For the same reason, Australian parrots' beaks have gotten 10 percent larger in the last 100 years.
Shapeshifting isn't the only way animals have adapted. A study found that 72 species of birds have begun to lay their eggs about a month earlier than they did about 120 years ago.
Some flowers are also blooming earlier in the year. When this happens, insects come out sooner. So, birds will lay their eggs early to make sure there are enough insects available to feed their young.
Other animals have adapted by migrating at different times of the year. This gives them access to food that they might not find during their typical migration times.

Problems can result from changes in animal behavior.

Habitat loss and lack of food have caused some animals to migrate to new areas to find food or shelter.

In some cases, this means animals have started to encounter humans more often.

For example, polar bears need to spend more time on dry land during summer because there is not enough ice in their habitats. On land, they look for new sources of food. That may include animals that belong to humans, such as pets or livestock. Polar bears also seek out and eat garbage.

Scientists are worried that encounters such as these could lead to wild animals being harmed by humans. Biologist Robert Rockwell says, "We're going to lose more polar bears due to gunfire than we are due to starvation."

Even without the threat of humans, animals migrating to new locations could create new competition for the areas' water and food. Animals native to these areas could lose out on resources that used to be abundant.

And new animals coming in could create scarcity in another habitat, leading to another cycle of animals entering unfamiliar habitats.

Chapter Four: What Can We Do?

Time is running out to help plants and animals. Up to 30 percent of species could be extinct by the year 2070.

One way to help is to eat a vegetarian or vegan diet. Not eating meat and dairy products helps lower emission levels, which helps keep places such as the Arctic and the Antarctic cold. That can help save penguins, polar bears, seals, and other animals.

Thanks for helping me switch these bulbs to lower-energy ones, kiddo.

Another way to help fight climate change is by keeping energy usage low. Using low-power bulbs, running appliances during non-peak hours, and using thermostats are all ways to help save energy.

Wait, Dad! We can't use that!

Reducing the use of pesticides is another easy way to help. That way, people produce fewer pesticides, which releases fewer greenhouse gases. And in areas where milkweed grows, not using pesticides on gardens helps keep this plant alive. That gives monarch butterflies a place to lay their eggs.

What might happen if endangered animals are saved? Would things go back to normal? Experts aren't sure.

Humans have taken over a lot of Earth's land for homes, businesses, and factories. If climate change slows and animal conservation is successful, animal populations could start bouncing back. But an increase in animal populations could mean that animals and humans would need to share more space.

If animal populations increase but their habitats have not grown back at the same rate, the result could also force animals into smaller spaces. This could create even more competition for food.

Climate change creates many problems for animals and the planet. Some people might think these problems are too big to solve. But even small actions can make a big difference.

Planting trees is a great way to help. The more trees Earth has, the more oxygen and less carbon dioxide are present in the air.

Write a letter to a congressperson about a topic that's important to you.

What are you going to write about?

I'm going to ask that we pass more laws to stop climate change. I want to help save animals.

Writing letters and emails to local, state, and federal government leaders is one way to demand action to protect the environment.

PROTEST FOR CLIMATE CHANGE
Saturday 12 P.M.

THERE IS NO PLANET B

Protests and marches are other ways for people to voice their opinions and to tell governments that change can't wait.

SOURCE NOTES

18–19 "Speech by President von der Leyen at the One Ocean Summit," *European Commission*, February 11, 2022, https://ec.europa.eu /commission/presscorner/detail/en/speech_22_962

24–25 Nina Dragicevic, "Polar Bears May Adapt to an Ice-Free Arctic, But They're Not Safe from Climate Change, Says Scientist," *CBC: The Nature of Things*, February 23, 2021, https://www.cbc.ca /documentaries/the-nature-of-things/polar bears-may-adapt-to-an-ice -free-arctic-but-they-re-not-safe-from-climate-change-says-scientist -1.5924442#:~:text=Things%C2%B7In%20Depth-,Polar%20bears%20 may%20adapt%20to%20an%20ice%2Dfree%20Arctic%2C%20but,put%20 them%20in%20harm%E2%80%99s%20way.

GLOSSARY

captivity: the state of being kept

climate change: long-term change in global temperatures

deforestation: clearing and cutting down of forests or parts of forests

emissions: things that are released into the air, such as gas

extinct: completely gone from Earth

global warming: the process that causes Earth to get hotter

greenhouse gases: gases in Earth's atmosphere that trap in heat

habitat: a place where an animal lives

predators: animals that hunt other animals

poaching: hunting or capturing wild animals illegally

FURTHER READING

Barr, Catherine. *Red Alert! Endangered Animals Around the World.* Watertown, MA: Charlesbridge, 2018.

Climate Kids
https://www.climatekids.org/

Clinton, Chelsea. *Disappear: 12 Endangered Species Across the Globe.* New York: Philomel, 2019.

Endangered Species: Kids Discover Online.
https://online.kidsdiscover.com/unit/endangered-species

NASA Climate Kids: Plants and Animals
https://climatekids.nasa.gov/menu/plants-and-animals/

INDEX